Purple Pride

by Christianne C. Jones

illustrated by Todd Ouren

Special thanks to our advisers for their expertise:

Linda Frichtel, Design Adjunct Faculty
Minneapolis College of Art & Design

Susan Kesselring, M.A., Literacy Educator
Rosemount–Apple Valley–Eagan (Minnesota) School District

VBC LIBRARY
119 SHAKE RAG RD.
CLINTON, AR 72031

DATE DUE

DISCARD

243899

PICTURE WINDOW BOOKS
Minneapolis, Minnesota

Editor: Jill Kalz
Designer: Amy Muehlenhardt
Page Production: Brandie Shoemaker
Art Director: Nathan Gassman
The illustrations in this book were created digitally.

Picture Window Books
5115 Excelsior Boulevard
Suite 232
Minneapolis, MN 55416
877-845-8392
www.picturewindowbooks.com

Copyright © 2007 by Picture Window Books
All rights reserved. No part of this book may be
reproduced without written permission from the
publisher. The publisher takes no responsibility
for the use of any of the materials or methods
described in this book, nor for the products thereof.

Printed in the United States of America.

Library of Congress Cataloging-in-Publication Data
Jones, Christianne C.
Purple pride / by Christianne C. Jones ; illustrated by
Todd Ouren.
p. cm. — (Know your colors)
Includes bibliographical references and index.
ISBN-13: 978-1-4048-3109-4 (library binding)
ISBN-10: 1-4048-3109-6 (library binding)
ISBN-13: 978-1-4048-3492-7 (paperback)
ISBN-10: 1-4048-3492-3 (paperback)
1. Purple—Juvenile literature. 2. Color—Juvenile literature.
3. Toy and movable books—Specimens. I. Ouren, Todd, ill.
II. Title.
QC495.5.J659 2007
535.6   2006027239

The world is filled with COLORS.

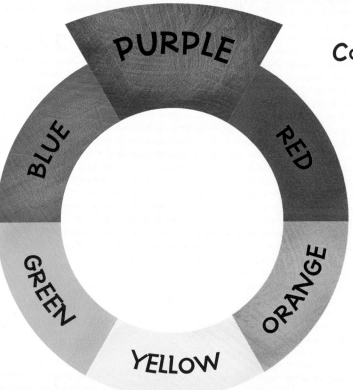

Colors are either primary or secondary. Red, yellow, and blue are primary colors. These are the colors that can't be made by mixing two other colors together. Orange, purple, and green are secondary colors. Secondary colors are made by mixing together two primary colors.

Primary colors   Secondary colors

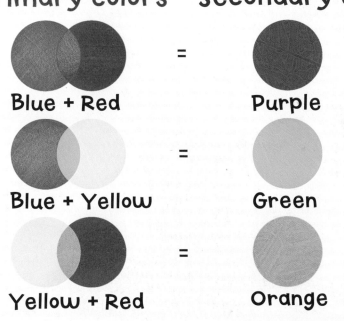

Blue + Red   =   Purple

Blue + Yellow   =   Green

Yellow + Red   =   Orange

Black and white are neutral colors. They are used to make other colors lighter or darker.

Keep your eyes open for colorful fun!

3

4

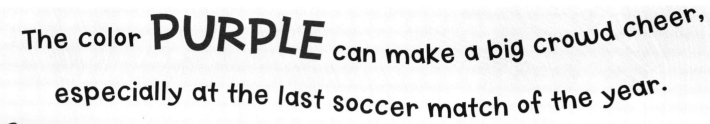

The color **PURPLE** can make a big crowd cheer, especially at the last soccer match of the year.

GOAL

5

Bold **PURPLE** uniforms run onto the field.

The new **PURPLE** mascot is revealed.

PANDAS

A bright **PURPLE** banner waves in the air.

11

A lucky PURPLE cap is fun to wear.

12

14

A cold **PURPLE** drink is a refreshing treat.

Striped **PURPLE** shoes cover players' feet.

3

02:01

0

PANDAS

GUEST

The **PURPLE** scoreboard says our team will win soon.

Flashing **PURPLE** fireworks pop, sizzle, and boom.

243899

The match is done. It's time to go home.

Where else at the stadium does **PURPLE** roam?

MAKE A SECONDARY COLOR

WHAT YOU NEED:
- a clear bowl half full of water
- red food coloring
- blue food coloring
- a spoon

WHAT YOU DO:
1. Add a few drops of red food coloring to the water. Then, add a few drops of blue.
2. Use the spoon to stir the water to see what color you made!

TO LEARN MORE

AT THE LIBRARY
Gordon, Sharon. *Purple.* New York: Benchmark Books, 2005.

Schuette, Sarah L. *Purple.* Mankato, Minn.: A+ Books, 2003.

Yoon, Salina. *The Crayola Rainbow Colors Book.* New York: Little Simon, 2004.

ON THE WEB
FactHound offers a safe, fun way to find Web sites related to this book. All of the sites on FactHound have been researched by our staff.

1. Visit www.facthound.com
2. Type in this special code: 1404831096
3. Click on the FETCH IT button.

Your trusty FactHound will fetch the best sites for you!

FUN FACTS

- In some places in the world, purple is the color of wisdom and healing. In other places, purple stands for royalty.
- In some contests, a purple ribbon is the highest honor.
- The Purple Heart is a special medal. It is given to American soldiers who are hurt or killed in battle.
- Red, orange, and yellow are called warm colors. Blue, green, and purple are called cool colors.

Look for all of the books in the Know Your Colors series:

- Autumn Orange
- Big Red Farm
- Camping in Green
- Hello, Yellow!
- Purple Pride
- Splish, Splash, and Blue

24